CALIFORNIA

CRESCENT

INTRODUCTION

Ever since one wet January day in 1884 when a carpenter at John A. Sutter's Sawmill picked up a chunk of yellow metal and started one of history's great gold rushes, California has been to many the promised land; a land of unlimited opportunity.

People flocked to California in search of gold; they piled onto the railroads when the lines were first pushed into California; they walked, drove and

hitched into California when the citrus and grape industries called out for labor, when oil and natural gas were discovered, when Hollywood promised overnight stardom, when drought turned huge areas of the American southwest into a Dust Bowl, when shipyards and aircraft plants opened up thousands of new jobs.

In 1848 the population was estimated at 14,000; by the 1860s it was well on the

way to half a million and between 1860 and 1960 it doubled virtually every 20 years. California has long since overtaken New York as the most heavily populated member of the United States and is now approaching a figure of 20 million – roughly one in 20 of all Americans. By the year 2000 population pundits believe that that figure will have become one in five.

With this tremendous surge of manpower has come immense industrial muscle which, allied to the academic, artistic, scientific and commercial expertise attracted from around the world by unrivaled salaries and unsurpassed working conditions, has propelled

Sunshine and blue sky provide a constant background in the Golden State, against which are shown the graceful Club House of Silverado Golf Club **top far left,** *the fine grapes of the Napa Valley* **bottom far left,** *Oakland Bay Bridge, the world's largest steel bridge,* **left** *and Hollywood Boulevard, Los Angeles* **above.**

California into a unique position: only five nations of the world produce and sell more goods than does this one American state, and one of those nations is the United States itself.

"California", says Michael Davie in his book, *In the Future Now,** "is the only society ever founded on respect for money, which is one reason why it is now
*Hamish Hamilton, London, 1972

the richest segment of the surface of the globe, and why Californians are the richest people there have ever been."

But even with the strength of its people, even with their highly successful

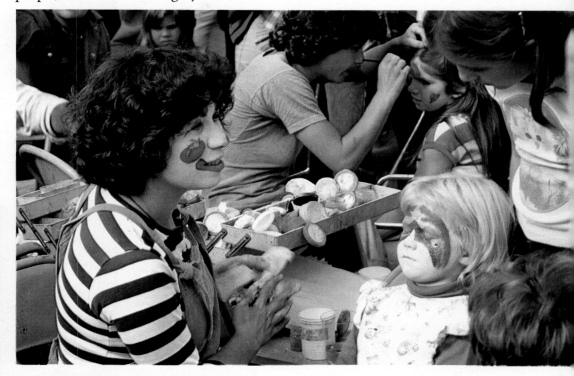

Face painting is one of the many events at the exciting Pumpkin Festival held in Half Moon Bay, San Mateo County **above.**

"Work hard, play hard" philosophy, it is doubtful if California would have made such a mark on the world, or such wealth for its citizens, without its abundant natural attributes.

Its magnificent climate is certainly one. The coastal strip – roughly 2 percent of the State and where 94 percent of the people live – luxuriates in temperatures that rarely exceed 90 degrees F (32 degrees C) or fall to freezing point. Rainfall is moderate, about 20 inches a year in San Francisco, for instance. Yet north of that city there are areas that are deluged by as much as 180 inches a year. In the far south, summer temperatures in the desert areas hit Sahara heights, while the peaks of the Sierra Nevadas often experience temperatures as low as those of the Arctic.

The state's 158,000 square miles contain the impressive mountain ranges of the Sierra Nevada, as well as forests, deserts, lakes and 1,200 miles of the most beautiful coastal scenery to be seen anywhere, now protected by the extensive powers of a specially appointed Coastal Commission.

INTRODUCTION

Within less than 100 miles of each other in California lie the highest and lowest points of mainland USA – Mt Whitney at 14,494 feet, and Death Valley, 282 feet below sea level at its lowest point. The Valley was known to Red Indian tribes for generations, but was unknown to white man until a party of prospectors seeking a shortcut to the gold fields stumbled upon it. It is now a national monument.

Mt Whitney is part of the Sierra Nevada range that runs south for 430 miles from Lassen Peak to the fringes of Los Angeles. It is quite an experience for the first-time visitor to Los Angeles to drive along Melrose Avenue in a temperature of 80 degrees F or more, while the snow capped peaks of the Sierras glint a dazzling white in the

One of California's main features is the spectacular and contrasting scenery to be found in places like the barren Zabriskie Point **above,**

the Devils Golf Course **left,** *both in Death Valley National Monument. The remains of a volcanic mountain rise 1,200 feet from the valley floor in Pinnacles National Monument* **bottom right,** *and dense forests and towering peaks provide unimaginable beauty in the Yosemite National Park* **above right.**

summer sky to the north.

High up in the Sierras, near the state border with Nevada, is one of the most beautiful of America's lakes, Lake Tahoe, more than 6,000 feet above sea level, nearly 200 square miles in area and, at a depth of 1,600 feet, one of the world's deepest. It is now a superbly developed resort area with Olympic standard skiing facilities, casinos, cabarets and nightclubs where the finest of America's entertainers regularly appear.

INTRODUCTION

The state's main desert areas are the Colorado in the south west where fewer than three inches of rain fall in a year and some of the world's highest temperatures have been recorded and the Mojave Desert, where apart from a few military installations, aviation and rocket ranges and the occasional intrepid explorer, the desert's 25,000 square miles are as unsullied by human endeavor as on the day they were created (although efforts were made recently to establish a nuclear power plant there!).

California's forests, however, *have* suffered from the arrival of the settler. The redwood forests, for instance, where many of these magnificent trees are up to 2,000 years old and tower 300 feet, now

cover less than 10 percent of their former territory. Recent, far-reaching state legislation ensures there will be no further inroads into one of California's great legacies.

The arrival of settlers, and the inevitable erosion of some of the state's natural beauty and riches, dates from the discovery of gold. But California's history, as far as the white man is concerned, goes back another century. The Spaniards can claim to have discovered California – then occupied by scattered Red Indian tribes – and by the late 18th century Franciscan friars were establishing missions along the Pacific coasts, the first at San Diego in 1769. The Spaniards were eventually

Missions are part of California's heritage and the old mission at San Juan Bautista **right** *is the State's largest church. Mission San Francisco Solano* **above right,** *which dates from 1832, is situated in the Sonoma Valley. Preserved in the State Historic Park in Napa Valley is the Bale Grist Mill* **top** *while Ports O'Call in San Pedro along the main channel of Los Angeles Harbor recaptures the atmosphere of a New England seacoast village* **above.**

ousted by the Mexicans, leaving behind little more than their architecture and place names. In 1846, the emergent United States defeated Mexico and huge tracts of land, including much of modern California, became American, and in 1850 California became the 31st state of the Union.

At this time, of course, gold was still the major preoccupation of the State's immigrants; it had lured them into San Francisco by boat from all over Europe, as well as in more than 6,000 wagons on the hazardous overland trail from the Midwest and the east, where cholera claimed

more victims than hostile Indian tribes or extremes of climate and terrain.

Chinese faces became increasingly seen among the predominantly Anglo-Saxon workers and they stayed to form the origins of the Chinese communities in California today. Fifteen years later the railroads were dynamiting through the Rockies with the aid of hundreds of Irish laborers who also stayed on and, with the Italians and French, made San Francisco their new home.

The former gold mining town of Julian pictured **below right and above** *lies in San Diego's back country and has been preserved very much as it was. The town retains the flavor of the heady days of the gold rush. The old methods of panning for gold are still demonstrated and visitors can try their hand, perhaps feeling a little of the excitement of "gold-fever"!*

Top right *is Whaler's Wharf, also in San Pedro, where fishing boats, yachts and tuna clippers fill the harbor, and* **center right** *is a different view of the peaceful mission at San Juan Bautista.*

SAN FRANCISCO

The city had been founded only a century before, in 1776 when a landing was made in the Bay by a Spanish expedition. Until California entered the Union, San Francisco was little more than a Spanish settlement, but in the 1830s the first American homes and ranches were established on the slopes of the 43 hills. With the Gold Rush all that changed, and the Bay suddenly had to cope with vessels arriving daily from all parts. Wharves were hastily erected to cope with them; the hillsides suddenly sprouted tents and shanties, and the shrewder settlers opened up bars and gambling houses to part the prospectors from their golden gains.

Within ten years of the first find, San Francisco's 1845 population of about 300 had swelled to nearly 60,000, and the city had already established a character of its own. There was a Chinatown; North Beach was where the Italians set up home, and the Barbary Coast provided nightlife. There was also a commercial center and the peripheral services needed for the life style spawned by the Gold Rush.

In the 1860s, oil replaced gold as the Californian bonanza and, until the end of the century, San Francisco's population and city development expanded fast. Then, in the course of a few minutes early on the morning of April 18, 1906, life as San Francisco knew it came to an end. An initial two-minute earthquake tremor bowled over buildings and sparked off fires that raged for three days across the city, killing more than 500 and, by destroying nearly 30,000 buildings, virtually razed the whole of the city's development.

As with the Great Fire of London, however, the disaster gave the City Fathers an opportunity to stamp out the unhygienic, cramped conditions caused by hasty, unplanned building and to reconstruct on far more generous lines. In less than 10 years the new San Francisco took shape, celebrated in 1915 by the Panama-Pacific Exposition.

Despite the steep hills which make up the peninsula, at whose northern extremity is the famous Golden Gate Bridge, the streets form an inflexible grid which sends some of them up hill and down dale in a series of ascents and descents

SAN FRANCISCO

reminiscent of a roller coaster. A popular location for car chases in police thriller movies, the streets also give riders of San Francisco cable cars some moments of breathtaking excitement as well as superb views of the Bay.

The cable cars are themselves symbols of a kind and, despite modern traffic conditions and more suitable means of public transport, no San Franciscan would part with them. Though no longer as numerous as in the past, the cable cars still run east and west along California Street and north to south along Powell and Hyde Streets, clanging their bells at every intersection and claiming a right-of-way that no one would dare dispute.

Market Street is a key street in the design of the city; running from south-west to northeast across the eastern side of the city, it forms an angle with Van Ness Avenue, which runs due north and

Oakland Bay Bridge **top,** *silhouetted against a spectacular sunset, links San Francisco and Oakland, its neighbor across the water. The City Hall* **above** *contrasts with the city's ultra modern buildings.*

south. Between the two streets is contained the liveliest and richest part of the city's life.

In the southern angle of the triangle lies the Civic Center, a spacious area laid out with lawns and parks among which rise dignified buildings where federal, state and city authorities carry out their responsibilities. During the day this is a quarter where people go about their business in the quiet and routine manner suited to civic surroundings, but even here the cheerful spirit of San Francisco comes to the fore from time to time. One of these times is in spring when the trees are in blossom and an open-air art show provides a colorful display of human ingenuity and imagination.

Art is very much a part of the Civic Center. Among its eight major buildings, which include the Renaissance style City Hall, is the War Memorial Opera House

SAN FRANCISCO

which is the home of the San Francisco Opera, the San Francisco Symphony Orchestra and the Ballet. Many fine artistic performances have taken place in the Opera House, but the most momentous event of all was the signing of the United Nations Charter there in 1945.

On gala nights, the Opera House still recalls some of the dazzle of the Belle Époque when famous singers like Tetrazzini entertained San Francisco society. In those rough pioneering days, when San Francisco possessed one of the toughest, bawdiest quarters of any city in America, it also stood out as a center of culture. The cultural side had been built up by the many Europeans who had come to San Francisco in search of a new life, and the foundation they laid is still basic in the city's life.

Famous for its sea-food, Fisherman's Wharf **above** *in the older part of the city is overlooked by the striking Transamerica pyramid* **left.** **Overleaf** *Night falls on Oakland Bay Bridge.*

The contrast between the two aspects of the city's life is in keeping with the paradoxical nature of San Francisco itself, much of whose charm today lies in the unexpected contrasts of its streets. Compare, for example, the character of the buildings around Union Square, the traditional center of the city, with those of Chinatown, only a few blocks away up Grant Avenue. At Union Square, and the surrounding Powell, Stockton, Geary and O'Farrell Streets, are the smartest shops and restaurants, jewelers, flower shops and flower stands along the sidewalks,

SAN FRANCISCO

reflecting the changing seasons in a riot of color. There is a certain formality about the shoppers here; the ladies often wear hats and the men stopping to buy a bouquet for one of them at the flower stalls are conventionally attired. Even Maiden Lane on the east side of the Square has forgotten its wicked past as the street of brothels and looks demure with its line of trees and little boutiques.

Chinatown is quite different. Here the buildings have an exotic sweep to them and the shop windows are festooned with Oriental goods, or if they are food shops, with shiny glazed ducks or strings of Chinese candies. Most of the faces peering into the windows with amazement and delight will be those of tourists, but even the San Franciscan can become a tourist from time to time as he explores his own city.

Another contrast nearby is Montgomery Street, a thoroughfare made to seem narrow by the office buildings that rise like the side of a concrete canyon into the sky. This is the Wall Street of the West and in and around it are the banks, insurance companies and brokerage firms

where business life hums all day long and sometimes into the night. Among the tall buildings are the Bank of America which rises to 779 feet in 52 stories, and the Wells Fargo Building slightly lower at 43 stories. The latter company played an important part in the business life of the early West when it transported the gold and silver which had brought fortune to the businessmen who supplied the prospectors' needs.

There is plenty of historical interest in this part of San Francisco, for this is where the first settlement began to grow. The very first house was built at Clay Street, when the settlement was still known as Yerba Buena, a name the Spaniards gave it because of the abundance of a sweet-smelling herb which grew there. Farther along Clay Street is Portsmouth Square where Captain John Montgomery planted the U.S. flag and claimed the land for the

The cable cars are a marvelous way to get around, and, as they travel at only 9½ miles per hour, the visitor will have plenty of opportunity to see the sights. The only city in the world with cable cars, they were introduced to prevent horses being overworked as they pulled heavy loads up and down the city's steep slopes.

United States in 1846. Perhaps it was this stirring event that appealed to the imagination of Robert Louis Stevenson, who liked to sit and dream in the grassy square when he lived in San Francisco.

A little farther north is a quarter which lives up to the paradox that is San Francisco; once it was the Barbary Coast, a name that has sounded round the world as a symbol of violence and vice. On the Barbary Coast, the roughest elements

SAN FRANCISCO

among the gold seekers, the sailors and the tough men who pioneered the West would gather to have a wild time. Prostitution was rife, with young Chinese girls pressed into the profession, and murders were so common that few of the perpetrators were brought to justice. Today the Barbary Coast is an area of smartly restored buildings and shops. A few blocks to the north is another paradox—the quarter known as North Beach though there is no sign of sea or sand. This is inhabited by San Francisco's peace-loving Italians, whose main concern appears to be to build a little Italy in the surrounding streets. Everywhere there are food shops, their counters laden with

Colorful figures like the clown-faced street musician **left** *bring life and character to the San Francisco streets.*

spaghetti, pizzas, cheeses, olives and all the other delicious ingredients of Italian cooking. Behind the counters stand the Italian ladies, looking as if they have just been transported from Naples and ready for an argument or a discussion about the quality of the products they sell.

This is one aspect of North Beach; another has echoes of the wicked old days. At Broadway and Columbus the night scene is one of flashing neon, sidewalk cafés, striptease parlors and jazz clubs. The famed San Francisco liberal spirit runs riot here, though today one does not walk in danger of one's life, or of being shanghaied and waking up a member of the crew on a ship bound for China.

North Beach is to San Francisco what Soho is to London or Montmartre to Paris: a place of entertainment with tourists in mind. The regular residents have them in mind, too, so here one finds little shops

San Francisco's geographical position and the city's development as the largest seaport on the West Coast combined to make it the "Gateway to the Orient." The result was "Chinatown" **remaining pictures these pages.**

where crafts are on sale and the craftsmen who make them live quiet working lives in the neighborhood.

To the southwest of the noisy, frenetic area around Columbus is the quiet, residential quarter of Nob Hill where two cable car routes cross. Near its summit, there are splendid views across to Russian Hill and beyond to Telegraph Hill with its

SAN FRANCISCO

tower which was built, some say, in the shape of a fire hose to commemorate the enthusiasm of Lillie Hitchcock Coit, its donor, for the city's firemen.

The triangle formed by Market Street and Van Ness Avenue opens out towards the Bay in the north: here there is a great sweep of quays stretching from the Oakland Bay Bridge on the east side to famous Fisherman's Wharf on the north. Beyond that along the coast lies the Golden Gate Bridge.

For the visitor, the north waterfront is the most fascinating part of San Francisco, as it is intended to be. Once busy with shipping, it decayed when the steamers' role as the main means of transport was taken over by rail and then by air transport; now it has been transformed into a playground in which memories of the past are cleverly linked with the practicalities of the present. At its western end lie two startling examples of the conversion of obsolete buildings. One is the chocolate factory at Ghirardelli Square. In the red brick buildings where chocolate was once produced, there are now art galleries, theaters, restaurants, and shops that sell jewelry and clothes imported from all over the world. The outdoor cafés are crowded in summer and part of the show is provided by the chefs who spin out paperthin pancakes or create ice cream sundaes as fantastic as the setting of Fisherman's Wharf.

The other converted building is The Cannery, a far cry now from the Del Monte factory where workers once packed the fruit from California orchards. Today's Cannery is a three-level shopping complex where goods can be bought ranging from primitive art to pet foods. From the top of the building there are fine views over city and harbor, including a sight of the notorious Alcatraz Island prison which once housed such infamous

The original Chinatown, built up around Grant Avenue, was destroyed in the devastating fire of 1906, but was subsequently rebuilt and is now the largest community of Chinese people living together with their own language, culture and laws, outside the Orient.

Alcatraz Island **left,** *now open to sightseers, was once the most dreaded penitentiary in the US. Fisherman's Wharf* **above** *teems with life, while the precipitous slopes of the hillside streets* **right** *afford wonderful views of the city and bay.*

criminals as Al Capone and Machine Gun Kelly. Alcatraz itself is another of the San Francisco paradoxes, for it never found enough of the tough tenants it was designed to house and so became an ordinary prison full of small-time crooks. The cost of maintaining them in the island fortress became prohibitive and the prison was phased out of use in the 1960's.

The fame of Fisherman's Wharf rests on many of the same reasons as that of Santa Lucia in Naples. Here is a dock on which the restaurants ply a busy trade and

the smell of frying and grilling fish fills the air. The view, when there is no fog, is sublime and stretches from the red structure of the Golden Gate Bridge to the land across the Bay. In the harbor, little boats and yachts bob at their anchors and along the sidewalks there are stalls that sell everything imaginable. As in Naples, the air is filled with the songs and music of itinerant musicians and romance is in the air.

A genuine touch of the old seafaring life remains at the eastern end of the Wharf where the *Balclutha*, a three-masted sailing ship that used to sail from Britain to San Francisco via Cape Horn, is moored and is now a museum. Nearby is another historic vessel, but this time a replica: the *Golden Hinde* of Sir Francis

23

SAN FRANCISCO

this part of the city, there is the Aquatic Park Maritime Museum which is packed with objects taken off old ships, including figureheads, anchors and binnacles.

From Aquatic Park starts one of the finest walks in San Francisco: along the Golden Gate Promenade west to Fort Point, which was built to defend the city and is now a museum. On the heights above the walk are some of the most expensive houses in San Francisco and on the sea before them some of their owners' luxurious yachts. Along this stretch of the waterfront are also the Presidio, where the Spaniards set up their garrison in 1776, and the weather-worn splendor of the Palace of Fine Arts, built as a temporary edifice for the 1915 Exhibition, which no one has had the heart to take down.

Although closely packed with its houses marching up and down the hills in close formation, San Francisco never seems constricted like other large cities. From its slopes there are always sweeping views across the bay or sea and overhead the sky stretches endlessly towards the mountains and over the Pacific. Nevertheless, the creators of the city have taken care to provide those open spaces essential in any urban area. The most important of these is Golden Gate Park, converted by John McLaren from a wild sweep of sand-dunes into a park that is the joy of all San Franciscans. During weekdays visitors can park their cars anywhere along the drives that traverse the park but on weekends, except for John Kennedy Drive, the pedestrian is king.

The western end of the park is fringed by the Pacific Ocean whose great waves crash along the beach beyond the Great Highway. At its eastern end Haight Street, of Haight Ashbury and Flower Children fame, connects with Market Street which runs through San Francisco to the Bay waterfront at Embarcadero. In the park there are bridle paths, bicycle tracks, lakes and museums. Buffalo and elk roam freely in a special area and by the M.H. de Young Museum, with its special wing that houses the Asian Art Collection of Avery Brundage, is a Japanese Tea garden. Every detail of the three-acre site has been carefully designed to simulate a Japanese Garden and includes a temple, a bridge,

Drake which was built in Devon only a few years ago and sailed across to America in an evocation of the original voyage.

There are still more ships to be found at the Hyde Street Pier, for those who feel nostalgic for the old days when ships were more than mere symbols of adventure. This is San Francisco's Maritime State

The Palace of Fine Arts **top** *contrasts with the high-rise office buildings of the Embarcadero Center* **above.** *This view of the city* **right** *illustrates the unusual location of San Francisco, being surrounded on three sides by water.*

Historic Park and along the length of the pier are schooners, ferry boats and a steam tug. To clinch the maritime character of

SAN FRANCISCO

gateways, a Buddha and even a teahouse where tea is served by Japanese ladies in national costume.

In another part of the park the atmosphere is very English, with a splendid white-painted iron and glass greenhouse like the one at Kew Gardens by the Thames, sitting elegantly amid the foliage.

The beautiful Golden Gate Park, once a wasteland of rolling dunes, contains such delights as the bronze Buddha **above** *and the exotic Japanese Tea Garden* **right.**

In the center of the city lies Twin Peaks, a tall hill with a 65-acre park which is a favorite viewpoint with visitors and residents. From here there is a bird's-eye view of the whole city, including the Bay and the Golden Gate and Oakland bridges, stretching away to the Marin shore in the north and to the island of Yerba Buena and then on to Oakland in the northeast. To the west lies the Pacific and to the south the spectacular coastline of Monterey and Big Sur.

From a high viewpoint such as this it is easy to see why the bridges feature so largely in San Francisco's mind; they are the lifelines between the city and the rest of the land around the Bay. Before they were built, all transport across the Bay was by ferryboat. The bridges gradually put the ferries out of business, though one has come back into operation in recent years.

The bridge connecting San Francisco to Oakland was completed in 1936 and today carries the commuter traffic from Oakland. The overall length of the bridge is eight and a quarter miles and it has a two-deck structure carrying one-way traffic on each level. At Yerba Buena Island, where it dives through a tunnel, there is a magnificent view of San Francisco for motorists who are traveling west; a view that is even more unforgettable at night.

Though Oakland Bay Bridge is a complex structure as well as the world's longest steel bridge, it is the Golden Gate Bridge, opened in 1937, that is the symbol

For the visitor, the sight of the sun setting over the Golden Gate Bridge **above** *must be a fitting end to a day spent discovering the many treasures of the city of San Francisco.* **Left** *is the ever-busy Oakland Bay Bridge.*

of San Francisco. The graceful silhouette of the bridge has appeared in millions of vacation photos and movies, and over thirty million vehicles cross it every year. To most people it is the most potent of all the images of San Francisco, representing a gateway to adventure and new ideas which, when the sea mist rolls in and wraps itself around the span, appears as two stairways leading skywards into an infinite space.

LOS ANGELES

For 60 years San Francisco was the major Californian city but by the 1920's it was being overtaken in size, and significance to the state economy, by its brash southern counterpart: Los Angeles. With around three million people, L.A. - as it is universally known – now has about four times the population of San Francisco. It was proclaimed by Father Crespi in 1769 when he accompanied the Spanish Expeditionary Force, led by Gaspar de Portola. The first mission, San Gabriel, was founded there in 1771 and with the addition of another, San Fernando, the resulting settlement grew large enough to be considered the chief town of Mexican California.

It is often said that Los Angeles is a city without a real heart, that central area in every large city in which its government, entertainment quarter, shopping areas and so on are contained: the hub which is the focus point of the city's life. There is some truth to this view, for Los Angeles has grown so rapidly in the decades since World War II that it cannot compare with world cities of comparable size that have had centuries in which to develop.

Another view is that Los Angeles is a city with several hearts, all beating powerfully in their respective locations and sending the lifeblood of the city coursing along the circulatory system of the freeways in a helter-skelter of vehicles with people who scurry about the city on business or pleasure.

This, too, is true and one glance at a map of the city, which stretches like a gargantuan tadpole – its head reaching over the Santa Monica Mountains into the San Fernando Valley to the north and its tail wiggling its way south to the port of

The flag of Los Angeles county flutters beneath the Stars and Stripes **right.** *Shimmering lights reflect the city's vibrant heart* **above.**

Los Angeles and Long Beach – will instantly reveal the diffuse nature of the community.

The historical eye of this monster's head is a small plaza with the unexpected atmosphere of an old Spanish village. This is where the Pueblo de Nuestra Senora la Reina de Los Angeles (the town of Our Lady, the Queen of the Angels) was founded by the Spaniards. Neglected for many years, the Pueblo has now become part of an area of 42 acres preserved as a State Historical landmark.

In the center of the square rises an old bandstand of the kind found in Latin American villages, around which the inhabitants usually promenade during

wine donated by the San Gabriel mission. Even that money was not enough to erect more than a very simple structure and over the years the weather has taken its toll on the adobe walls. There has been some restoration however, and in the interior much of the spirit which comforted and inspired the early settlers remains. The altar is of carved wood inset with paintings, and the painted ceiling and wooden pews are reminders of churches in old Spain. With the tall palms growing in its courtyard and its rebuilt belltower with three bells set in arches, the Church has retained for Los Angeles the character of its early days.

Another attractive reminder of the city's Spanish origins is found at Olvera

*Myriad lights gleam over the metropolis, and LA's exciting skyline comes alive **above, above right and right,** while the Crocker Bank towers provide a backdrop for the enchanting, colorful fountain **bottom far right.***

summer evenings. The same traditions are maintained in this quiet area of Los Angeles, almost the only place free of traffic. Bands play during the summer evenings and colorful Mexican fiestas are celebrated with mariachi groups filling the air with the sounds of guitars and providing a feast for the eye with their romantic Mexican sombreros and embroidered ponchos.

One of the oldest buildings in the Plaza is the old Mission Church, now known as the Plaza Church. This is one of a string of churches and missions built along the coast by the Spaniards in an attempt to colonize California. The Plaza Church began as a chapel for the settlers in 1784 and was rebuilt in 1822 on the proceeds of the sale of several barrels of

Street. Here is the oldest house in Los Angeles, the Avila Adobe, built in the original village in 1818, and the feeling of the street market that ran along the old main street is still to be found here today. Olvera Street is for pedestrians only; small shops with craftsmen at work line the street and musicians stroll amid the stalls on which hang embroidered shirts, scarves and leather belts, or step carefully around the piles of pottery displayed on the sidewalk. In the evenings, the lanterns glow and music fills the air, as do the odors of tacos and enchiladas which visitors order at take-out stalls or enjoy at the Mexican restaurants.

In the Pueblo there are also buildings from the city's early American period

when rich ranchers put up at the Pico House, the grandest hotel of its day boasting three stories and eight rooms, some with an article of bathroom furniture which was a novelty in the West in 1869 – a bathtub with hot water. There is also the Merced Theater where gala nights were packed with everyone of note in old Los Angeles.

In complete contrast to the Pueblo but close by it across the Hollywood Freeway, is the modern Civic Center. This complex of buildings is in a spacious area with parks and malls green with palms and evergreens. In it, the city authorities have tried to create that focal point which

the city lacks. The buildings are conventionally designed, according to the pattern of other civic centers in the U.S., and a good deal of the city's cultural life revolves about them.

One end is dominated by the City Hall which, until 1957, was the tallest building in the city, rising 32 stories and providing magnificent views on those rare smogless days.

Trotting is a popular night-time spectator sport **above two pictures,** *and the city's China-town sector abounds with interesting and unusual restaurants and shops* **center left. Top left** *Watts Towers are silhoutted against the evening sky. The Towers took 33 years to build and were completed in 1954.*

On the western end of the complex is another striking building, the Water and Power Building. This block by Albert C. Martin was built in 1964 and is particularly striking at night when the interior lighting shining through its abundant glass converts it into a huge sparkling cube that dominates the city.

Alongside the Water and Power Building is a black glass and marble building which is at the heart of the musical life of Los Angeles. This is the Dorothy Chandler Pavilion which was

built in 1964 and houses the Los Angeles Philharmonic Orchestra. Its auditorium seats 3250 people who attend performances of opera, ballet and music in its modern setting. The Pavilion is one of a trio of buildings for theatrical entertainments. The other two are the Mark Taper Forum, a smaller theater where much experimental drama is performed, and the Ahmanson Theater which can accommodate 2000 people for plays and musical shows.

In the West Coast cities of America the Orient has always had a foothold which was established first when the

Traffic makes its way along Western Avenue **left.** *One of the city's outstanding architectural designs is the Public Library* **above,** *flanked by the Union Bank and Bonaventure Hotel.*

Chinese arrived to work on the railway which was to link the two oceans that virtually surround the United States. Later, Japanese fruit farmers, attracted by stories of the fruitful valleys of the interior, came over to contribute their expertise in fruit cultivation.

Los Angeles' Chinatown lies to the north of the Pueblo and consists of a two-block area of Chinese buildings with large sloping roofs, covered in bright glazed

tiles, pagoda-like towers and colorful signs in Chinese characters advertising the presence of shops, restaurants and food markets. Like Little Tokyo, Los Angeles' second Oriental community which lies to the southeast of the City Hall, Chinatown is popular with the tourists who visit the city. Both areas also have their own commercial life which is part of the city's larger business life.

It is in downtown Los Angeles that major business development has taken place in recent years and here, to the southwest of the Civic Center, the high-rise buildings are beginning to take on the appearance of Italian cities of the Renaissance with their towers trying to outdo each other in height and magnificence. Formerly, this area, known as Bunker Hill, was the place where Los Angeles society resided but as they moved out the neighborhood became run down and is now going through a rebirth as a center of business and shopping.

Its center lies around Pershing Square, named after the World War I General but, surprisingly, possessing a statue of Beethoven, a relic of the days when this was the cultural center of the city and the Philharmonic Auditorium was situated here. Other reminders of the grand old

LOS ANGELES

days of this part of the city are the Biltmore Hotel, with its vast and imposing lobby and the murals of Giovanni Smeralda who also decorated Grand Central Station in New York in the nineteen twenties, and the Alexandria Hotel with its Tiffany ceilings which once looked down on everyone of note who visited Los Angeles. Today, both hotels are experiencing the same renaissance as the rest of this section of the city and the old glory has returned, enhanced by the nostalgia for the past felt by many present-day visitors.

Nearby, a startling contrast is provided by the modern Bonaventure Hotel, a vast complex of circular towers looking like the silos of some space station awaiting the arrival of visitors from another planet. Near it are other new giants like the 52-story Arco Plaza building and among them, looking like some Arabian nights castle, the Central Library.

This great storehouse of books, and there are more than four million of them, is the most important in the Western U.S.A. The building in which they are housed is very original, not to say extraordinary, in design. Bernard Goodhue, the architect who built it in 1925, was evidently a man of eclectic taste, for in its design one can identify Byzantine, Egyptian and Aztec influences. The exterior form of the building appears as a castle at street level and ends up as a mosaic-covered tent at the top.

Though purists may regard this type of architecture without much enthusiasm, it nevertheless reflects the spirit of the new society of America where the old cultural values of Europe, imported by a basically untutored population of immi-grants, is fused with the energy and dynamism of a people establishing a new world with the roots of the old.

This is the basis of much of the fanciful architecture of that home of fantasy, Hollywood, which in its film sets,

its restaurants, burger palaces and even in the homes of the stars themselves, presents a rich mixture of contrasting styles.

The tradition was established early on by film-maker D. W. Griffiths who, in his epic *Intolerance,* mixed Babylonian, Egyptian, Indian and other styles in an epic set which has never been equaled. Today, the architecture of the fantastic is everywhere: in Mann's (formerly Grauman's) Theater where the stars left their hand and footprints in the concrete in front of the strange South Sea Island/Chinese/Mexican-style movie house; in the Brown Derby's hemispherical architecture; or in the innumerable eating houses decked out as Hawaiian huts, Chinese temples or Aztec palaces.

The Post Office **far left,** *Mark Taper Forum* **below** *and the Civic Center Mall* **left** *are just three examples of the excitingly different architecture in Los Angeles. Intricately patterned and ornamented, the ceiling and globe* **right** *can be found in the Public Library, one of the best-stocked in the world.*

LOS ANGELES

The neighborhood of Watts, in which resides the majority of L.A.'s black population, was the scene of violent rioting one hot summer not long ago, and also contains one of the most remarkable examples of monumental folk art in the world. This consists of three conical towers built of wire rods and concrete and decorated with ceramics, shells and pieces of glass. It was built singlehandedly by Simon Rodia who dedicated himself to this labor of love for thirty-three years and, having finished it, left Los Angeles and his life's work behind without fuss. At

One of the most beautiful and wealthy areas of California is Beverley Hills, home of many famous movie stars **right.** *Pasadena's charming City Hall is pictured* **above.**

first, the city authorities intended to demolish this folly, but its artistic merit was recognized by the public, who opposed its destruction and saved it for posterity as a truly remarkable city monument.

Just as amazing, though because of its familiarity no one would term it so, is Dodgers Stadium in Elysian Park to the north of the city center. This is the home of the Dodgers baseball team, formerly of Brooklyn. It is a vast diamond whose terraces hold 56,000 seats with unobstructed views of the game. Around the stadium are giant parking lots which can accommodate the cars of the spectators who number more than two and a half million each season.

Sport is an important aspect of Los Angeles life, and one of the places where Los Angelenos exercise is 4064-acre Griffith Park. This is one of the largest city parks in the United States and on a fine weekend is used by over 50,000 people who can ride, hike, listen to music, study

the bird life in the Sanctuary or the plants in Fern Dell. All the flora and fauna of the park are on show at the Fern Dell Nature Museum, a favorite starting place for walkers in the vast park and one which vies in popularity with the Los Angeles Zoo, another of the park's attractions.

At the Zoo, the animals are in the open, their freedom limited only by moats and natural obstructions and their habitats

Hollywood Bowl **above,** *with its perfect acoustics, draws thousands of music lovers.*

are made to resemble those of their native terrains. There is also a childrens' Zoo, with such attractions as the Prairie Dog Colony, Mouse House and Baby Elephant compound.

Southwest of the hub of the city is another sports center at Exposition Park. Here is the Memorial Coliseum built for the 1932 Olympics, which seats over 100,000 people. The Universities of Los Angeles and California play their football games at the Coliseum and there are track meets and other shows such as rodeos and parades. Nearby is an indoor Sports Arena where boxing matches, tennis champion-ships, basketball games, and other events take place.

Leisure pursuits of Los Angelenos are not solely devoted to sporting activity, however, and on any weekend the museums are full of people. The Museum of Art, built in 1965, is one of the largest in the U.S.A. and is built over the tar pits in Hancock Park, an area where the bones of prehistoric creatures who died in the pits have been found and recreated in lifelike models. Although a newcomer to the world of art collections, the Museum has some fine paintings and sculptures, including the dramatic Rodin statue of Balzac. Other collections are the result of private patronage. For example, the Huntington Library, which has one of the largest collections of rare books and manuscripts in the world, was bequeathed to the public by H.E. Huntington, a tycoon and collector of both art and books. One of the few copies of the famous Gutenberg Bible is here and so is a first folio of Shakespeare. There are also some fine examples of British eighteenth-century painters, such as Lawrence and Gainsborough.

Another extraordinary private collec-tion is the one left by J. Paul Getty, popularly thought of as the richest man in the world. The Getty Collection at Santa

Reflecting pools ring the Los Angeles County Art Museum **above,** *while tranquil pools mirror the J Paul Getty Museum* **left, top left and right.**

Monica specializes in Greek and Roman sculpture and Dutch and Italian painters. There are also tapestries and furniture in this million-dollar museum and a fullsize model of the Villa dei Papyri which was unearthed from the ashes in which it was buried at Herculaneum following the eruption of Vesuvius in AD 79.

Whether by chance or because of its association with the motion picture industry, Los Angeles and its surrounding country are abundantly supplied with

unusual or off-beat entertainments and attractions. Many of these are scattered about the rambling city; most are easily accessible if not centrally situated. Among them are farms and animal breeding establishments, mock villages of the Old West, botanical gardens and one of the world's most famous observatories.

To the northwest, on the outer edges of the city and on the San Diego Freeway, are the Busch Gardens, a beautiful park with lakes on which one can take boat trips and view waterfalls and exotic aquatic birds. There are endless sideshows besides and one of the unusual excursions is a monorail tour of the Anheuser Busch brewery which owns the park.

Farther east lie the San Gabriel mountains. Atop Mount Wilson is the famous Observatory, with its powerful 100-inch Hooker telescope camera which has probed into millions of light years of space in an effort to unravel the mystery of the universe.

Directly below the mountain lie the Arboretum Botanical Gardens, created on an old ranch and now a horticultural center, and the California Institute of Technology, which is one of the world's leading educational establishments for science and engineering.

To get to these places of leisure or, indeed, to their work Los Angelenos must commute.

The scattered nature of the city of Los Angeles, which overlaps into the county of Los Angeles and surrounding counties,

LOS ANGELES

has led to the development of a sophisticated freeway system providing rapid travel from one area of Los Angeles to another. This has encouraged 90% of Los Angelenos to use their own vehicles instead of public transport, and has created traffic problems of considerable proportions which the administration has had to deal with by providing still more freeways and parking facilities.

Few homes in Los Angeles city are farther than four miles from a freeway and the traffic is intense. Moreover, Los Angeles receives over 20 million people a year through its international airport, who add to the already high number of urban travelers.

Traffic is just one problem which has grown out of the successful industrial and

For visitors to Los Angeles, there is always a multitude of ways to fill the long, warm days as these pages show – cycling, fishing, rides on a gold train, chess – as well as the fabulous sights in and around this vital city.

The effect of the smog on the health of the population has been severe, causing an increase in cardiac deaths and in lung diseases, while agriculture, already reduced by the take-over of farming land by urban development, has decreased.

With the prospect of the population continuing to increase into the 1980s the administration is concerned that the city should not suffer irreparable damage from the circumstances in which it finds itself. But the administration has problems of its own.

The administrative structure of the city and county is a tangled web of overlapping agencies which confuse the lines of authority and, therefore, action. In

Sunny, pleasure-filled Los Angeles has long drawn visitors to this dynamic metropolis where the excitement of the city is ever evident and the fun of "The Big Orange" is always ready to be tasted.

business development of the city. Others are sewage and waste disposal, but worse than either of these is smog.

It is ironic that one of the reasons why two of Los Angeles' major industries moved to the county was because it had clear air and sunshine. For the film industry, this meant the economy of location shooting instead of having to make expensive indoor sets; for the aircraft industry it provided ideal conditions for flying and testing aircraft. Today, they would both choose somewhere else to go, for the combination of fumes from factory chimneys and the hot sun produces a smog for which Los Angeles is notorious.

many cases the city has duplicated services, while in other cases departments are almost autonomous. In these circumstances, the city's development is too much the result of the enterprise of individuals who put profit before the interests of the community as a whole. Too often this has led to the despoiling of the countryside in such formerly beautiful areas as the Santa Monica Mountains and the San Fernando Valley.

In time, if Los Angeles continues to exist, it may become a city in the traditional European sense, but even the great cities have been subjected to extensive destruction and rebuilding to give them the form in which we see them today. Paris, for example, was rebuilt by Henry IV as well by Napoleon and Baron Haussman. In Los Angeles, the threat of

Fiesta Village, with its vibrant Mexican atmosphere, provides an opportunity for visitors to ride on the thrilling Mexican Whip, the Fiesta Wheel and the Happy Sombrero Ride **left and top left.** *The beautiful Santa Anita Park Racetrack in Arcadia is set in a superb location at the foot of the San Gabriel Mountains* **above.** *The popularity of the racetrack is not just because of the location, however. The course is patronized by many celebrities!*

destruction is ever-present with the San Andreas fault, a major cause of earthquakes, a mere 30 miles away from the city center. Perhaps it is this as much as anything else that gives Los Angeles a slightly transient character, as if the population might at any moment move away as quickly as it arrived, and endows it with a talent for living in the present with an intensity that is wholly its own.

HOLLYWOOD

The most famous 'suburb' in the world, Hollywood, was established at the turn of the century by a God-fearing tee-totaller, whose aim was to provide housing for farmers and other folk who were arriving in Los Angeles.

At around the same time, the film industry was beginning, albeit falteringly, in New York. However, restrictions imposed by the patent holders of the new film-making apparatus drove some independent producers to California to begin work in a studio on Sunset Boulevard.

These were the days before the Los Angeles smog, and the producers found the weather perfect for outdoor filming, obviating the need for building expensive sets. They started to turn out films that spread the name of Hollywood throughout the world. With the development of the studios, sophisticated techniques were used to create box-office hits. Also created was the star system. Actors and actresses were groomed for stardom, the best

writers in the land were engaged to write the scripts, and every aspect of the job of film-making became a specialized technology.

The studios, under the dictatorship of the film producers and financiers, employed publicists who ensured that the movie-goers were constantly reminded of everything that happened in the movie kingdom. Stars' lives became as familiar as those of the public's own families. The stars eventually rebelled against the

power of the movie moguls, however, and began to form their own film companies, confident of the appeal of their names.

Hollywood's attraction for tourists has again been revived by its new success as a television film production center, which brings thousands of visitors every year.

West along Hollywood Boulevard is Highland Avenue which leads to the Hollywood Bowl, the great amphitheatre in the hills where the Los Angeles

William Hearst's exquisite San Simeon estate **previous pages** *is now a state historical monument. Hollywood,* **these pages,** *attracts hundreds of visitors every week to see the sets, homes, models and hopefully the stars of this huge industry. Some of the larger Studios offer guided tours where guests can see at first hand the "behind the scenes" effects that are so realistic on film. Hollywood Boulevard* **right** *is the home of Mann's (formerly Grauman's) Chinese Theater, where the footprints and autographs of Hollywood's "greats" are immortalized in concrete* **above.**

Philharmonic holds its summer concerts 'under the stars' and which is crowded every Easter for the impressive Easter Sunrise Service.

Near Highland Avenue is the famous Wax Museum, where stars like Marilyn

Monroe and Clark Gable are depicted – frozen in a typical pose. The Museum also holds some of the props used in famous movies. Sunset Boulevard, associated in movie-goers' minds with the film starring Gloria Swanson, runs parallel to Hollywood Boulevard, cutting through to Beverley Hills. This fabulously wealthy area is the home of the movie stars, containing picturesque glens, canyons and hillsides, and studded with beautiful houses. The peace and tranquillity of this area is occasionally broken by the 'star-spotters'; coach-loads of tourists anxious to know which famous personality lives in which mansion!

To the south of Los Angeles is one of the major attractions of California, the world famous Disneyland.

Disneyland was Walt Disney's special dream more than twenty years before it became a reality. His name had already been established in the film world, but he was always thinking of new projects. The

The magic of Disneyland is illustrated by the expressions on the faces of the children, as they meet yet another of their favorite cartoon characters.

concept of Disneyland occurred to him when his two daughters were young, for there were very few suitable places of amusement for children at that time. He had the idea of building a 'magical little park' on two acres of land next to his Burbank Studios, with pony rides, a train, statues of his well-known and loved cartoon characters, and 'singing waterfalls'. Most of all, it would be a place devoted to family entertainment.

World War II interrupted his plans, but these were resumed shortly after the war ended. However, the original concept had now outgrown the area alongside his studios, and he assigned a team to seek out an appropriate piece of land. Eventually a site was found, in Orange County, an up and coming area served by the new, multi-laned Santa Ana Freeway. Disney bought 160 acres adjacent to the Freeway, but he realized that a huge amount of capital would be needed to develop the site. Financiers had little faith in the project, so

DISNEYLAND

he and his brother Roy borrowed as much as they could, and Walt Disney sold his vacation home, at a loss, and borrowed against life insurance policies.

He then set up an organization called WED Enterprises, which comprised artists, engineers, architects, designers, sculptors and special effects men – the majority chosen from his own and other motion picture studios – whose expertise and skill would realize the 'Disney Dream'.

Disneyland began to take shape. Disney described how he envisaged the park: "Physically Disneyland would be a small world in itself – it would encompass the essence of the things that were good and true in American life. It would reflect the faith and challenge of the future, the entertainment, the interest in intelligently

presented facts, the stimulation of the imagination, the standards of health and achievement, and above all, a sense of strength, contentment and well-being."

The scale of the Park was to be slightly less than life-size, so that children would not be overwhelmed, and the impression would be of friendliness and warmth. Plans were made for five different themed areas, each complementing the other, which would provide the visitor with total involvement in a sequence of events, along a skilfully designed route, ensuring that no facet of the story would be missed.

The five areas commenced with Main Street, a recreation of turn-of-the-century America. At the end of Main Street, the other areas fanned out. Adventureland was where the visitor could take part in a true-to-life safari, with tropical rivers, through lush jungles reminiscent of Africa and Asia, and where realistic-looking animals moved in the waters and along the banks.

Another area was Frontierland, where visitors were able to cruise on a Mississippi sternwheeler, or take a log raft or canoe to the exciting Tom Sawyer Island. The lusty days of the "Wild West" would be recreated in the atmosphere of the Golden Horseshoe Saloon.

Fantasyland included Disney's famous characters, like Mickey Mouse and Donald Duck, who "came to life" under the shadow of Snow White's enchanting castle.

The final area was Tomorrowland, where the attractions were designed "to

The largest attraction in California, Disneyland has so many exciting things to do and see in the themed lands of Main Street, Adventureland, New Orleans Square, Bear Country, Frontierland, Fantasyland and Tomorrowland, with their fun-packed special entertainments, guaranteed to keep the young wide-eyed and the adults spellbound.
From the fantastic to the magnificent – the rugged Big Sur coastline **overleaf** *at Bixby Creek.*

give an opportunity to participate in adventures which are a living blueprint of our future."

Plans completed, construction began

on July 16th 1954 and the project was finished a year and a day after. On July 17th 1955, Disneyland was officially opened, and 30,000 guests were there to witness the excitement of the day.

"I don't want the public to see the world they live in while they're in the Park," Walt Disney said. "I want them to

feel they are in another world." And with that, Walt Disney dedicated Disneyland.

The success of Disneyland has been assured, with millions of visitors having passed through the gates since 1955, and a continual increase in the number of attractions, making it one of America's top tourist spots.

Now a city with a population of just over a quarter of a million, Sacramento provides a step back in time to the days of the Gold Rush. A twenty-eight acre section of the city, Old Sacramento, recaptures the atmosphere of the mid 1800's frontier, with restored buildings, wagons and "watering holes." The city also contains Sutter House and Fort, reconstructed in the 1890's, which played a major role in the gold rush days.

Waterfalls, tranquil lakes, dense forests, towering cliffs and an abundance of wildlife make the Yosemite National Park a place of enchantment and stunning beauty. The Park was created when huge blocks of granite, formed beneath the earth's surface, buckled and lifted. The result is breathtaking.

Sacramento has emerged as an important agricultural center, its rich valley producing grain, vegetables, cotton, rice and sugar. Many smaller ranches have become vineyards, citrus groves and orchards, and dairy cattle and livestock graze in the peaceful valley. A far cry from the bustle and excitement of the Gold Rush!

Despite their size and significance, neither Los Angeles nor San Francisco is the State capital. That honor belongs to Sacramento, the cradle of California, where Marshall, the carpenter at Sutter's Sawmill, picked up the chunk of yellow metal on that rainy day in 1884. Sacramento's Capitol Building, housing the State legislature, was built in 1861 and its archives and library hold in their files the enthralling and dramatic history of California.

As well as the cosmopolitan cities and the varied and interesting towns, California boasts some of the most beautiful, contrasting scenery in the world. Its coastline stretches for twelve hundred miles, yet only a small part is visited. The northern beaches are uncrowded, quiet, but always spectacular. The Monterey

MONTEREY & CARMEL

peninsula, although attracting many tourists, never appears crowded. This is one of California's most scenic areas, dominated by miles of rocky coastline, white sandy beaches and acres of woodland. The area was named in honor of the Count of Monte Rey, Viceroy of Mexico, by a visiting explorer in 1602. It was not until 1770, however, when a Franciscan mission was established, that the area was settled. Shortly after, it became the Mexican capital, and for a brief time, the American capital of California.

Once a successful fishing port, the peninsula now has a thriving tourist industry. Even so, the area has managed to escape becoming "touristy," and offers a relaxed, comfortable pace.

Winding its way through pine forests, groves of Monterey cypress and the Del Monte Forest is the spectacular 17 Mile Drive. This magnificent route runs along the coastline between Carmel and Monterey, past brilliant white beaches, craggy inlets and an abundance of plants and trees. The road overlooks Point Joe, where many ships have been wrecked over the years when sailors have mistaken it for the entrance to Monterey Bay, and met with turbulent waters. The shoreline is the home of numerous seabirds and colonies of sealions, and the sea otter, once thought to be extinct in California, has returned to the State. One of six golf courses along the drive, the Pebble Beach Golf Course appeals to the more confident golfer, with the seventh hole almost completely surrounded by water.

Slightly more precarious is the drive along State Highway 1, as it weaves its way along the rugged Carmel-Big Sur coastline. The highway passes three large State parks and crosses the Bixby Creek Bridge to the town of Big Sur. Bixby Creek, one of the world's highest highway bridges, arches 260 feet above the creek bed, and overlooks a magnificent seascape. The Point Sur lighthouse, which can be seen from the bridge, stands on a headland of rock, and the light, flashing every fifteen seconds, is visible for twenty-five miles out at sea.

Carmel, at the peninsula's southern base, is a forest village which has attracted

The spectacular scenery of the Monterey coastline is shown on these pages. The scenic 17-Mile Drive curves past the Lone Cypress **left,** *while State Highway 1 winds over Bixby Creek* **right** *and in and out of the Coast Range* **top left.** *Golfers brave the hazards of the seventh hole of Pebble Beach Golf course* **top,** *and the dramatic sunset silhouettes Pigeon Point Lighthouse* **above.**

artists, sculptors, writers and weavers, all the while remaining totally unspoilt.

A shopper's paradise, the town has many clothes and craft shops, and the work of its artists is exhibited at local galleries. Most of the visitors make a pilgrimage to the church and mission buildings, founded in 1771 by Father Serra, and now carefully preserved. Carmel's curving beaches are beautiful, but the waters of the bay are extremely cold, and not conducive to swimming!

Monterey itself retains a 19th century air, and Cannery Row, the street that inspired John Steinbeck's book of the same name, still harbors the old canneries as monuments to the sardines that mysteriously disappeared from the bay in the late 1940s. Steinbeck described Cannery Row as "a poem, a stink, a grating noise." A description no longer true, as the street is brimming with art galleries, antique shops and restaurants.

William Randolph Hearst, the publishing giant, shared Steinbeck's feeling for Monterey, and chose the crest of one of the Santa Lucia Mountains in the peninsula – "The Enchanted Hill" – for his home. The castle-like mansion is now a State Historical Monument, open to the public, exhibiting fine collections of antiques, tapestries, Roman mosaics and wood carvings.

SOUTHERN CALIFORNIA

The coastline of Southern California holds a different appeal. Miles and miles of wide, sandy beaches attract thousands of city-dwellers on summer weekends, offering such pleasures as surfing, snorkeling, scuba diving, swimming, boating and fishing. The crescent-shaped Santa Monica Bay abounds with different beaches, each holding its own special appeal.

One of the most unusual sights along the coast of Southern California must be a retired Cunard Liner, the Queen Mary. This British passenger ship is now moored in Long Beach and is open for tours of her five decks. She is also used as a restaurant and as a floating hotel.

Marineland, the world's largest

An unusual sight at Long Beach, Los Angeles, is the retired liner, the Queen Mary **left,** *now a floating museum. Southern California's beaches attract thousands of visitors to their long, golden sands. Venice* **top left** *is an oceanside community south of Santa Monica, and resembles its namesake in Italy.*

oceanarium, is sited at the southwest tip of the Palos Verdes Peninsula. Here you can see a "killer whale" leap up to eighteen feet out of the water and grab a fish from its trainer, or a pair of dolphins leaping in tandem, or turtles, giant bass, sharks and many other fish being hand fed by a diver – watched by an audience through their tank's 170 windows.

Cross the mountains surrounding Los Angeles, heading north east, and you will face another of the State's contrasts – the desert.

The vast Mojave Desert stretches from the San Gabriel and San Bernadino mountains to Death Valley and south eastern Nevada. Although some parts have never been fully explored, the

Shamu, the killer whale, goes through his routine **left, above left and above,** *to the delight of the crowd. This magnificent, three-ton creature can leap up to 24 feet out of the water.*

Mojave is generally well-served with roads and pipelines, and desert cities are springing up, like Barstow, Daggett and the resort town of Apple Valley.

The northern part of the desert is dotted with mines – from gold, tungsten and silver to salt and borax. Traveling into

DEATH VALLEY

Death Valley via the Wildrose Canyon provides a wonderful view of the Trona Pinnacles. An example of the strange formations to be found in the desert, these spires are believed to have been formed from algae of an ancient sea.

A kaleidoscope of colors, Death Valley is a mixture of shifting sand dunes, clay hills, salt flats and the lava-topped Black Mountains. Oxidation of the ores contained in this range has produced the variety of colors, from pale green to rose pink. The effect is heightened by the sun as it moves across the heavens, high-lighting the different formations.

Seen against a backdrop of snow-capped peaks is Mono Lake **previous pages,** *contrasting sharply with the ever-shifting sands of Death Valley* **left. Above** *is one of the huge variety of cacti found in the desert.*

Nowhere are the contrasts of the desert more keenly observed than at Badwater, the lowest point in the Western Hemisphere at 282 feet below sea level. Towering above the salty pools, which are often crusted over, is Dante's View, on the crest of the Black Mountains, the most spectacular viewpoint in Death Valley, at 5,775 feet.

It is hard to imagine the existence of life in the extremes of the desert. However, life forms have managed to adapt and thrive. Species like snakes and lizards, coyotes, squirrels and jackrabbits, and various types of mice and rats, seem to exist quite happily, emerging from their homes at night only. Even more surprising is the abundance of plant life. A mass of color covers the desert floor in spring, after the winter rains. Yellow, pink, red and white – the variety seems almost endless. Only the central salt flats are barren of both animal and plant life.

The diversity of the Golden State is practically unbelievable – rich and fertile valleys, bleak, harsh coastline, white curving bays, spectacular mountain ranges and barren, inhospitable plains. All these features and more have made California one of the most attractive, and certainly the most popular, states of America. This

The sun sets over the ocean at Monterey **top,** *and rises over a snowy landscape at Lake Tahoe* **above.**

popularity, however, has created its own problems. Concrete highways, skyscrapers of steel and glass, and the smog lying in the ever-expanding towns and cities are a sad reminder of 20th century progress. It has been calculated that in the early 1980's Californians will own something in the region of 20 million cars, carried by 4,000 miles of multi-lane freeways. Pressure groups have been formed to protest against the rapid changes enforced by pollution, high technology, freeways and many other subjects. Luckily, the State is aware of the growing concern of Californians that inevitable progress does not destroy the very quality of life. New legislation has been passed to ensure that parks, forest areas and beauty spots are protected, thus safeguarding California's natural heritage for future generations – essential for the preservation of the Golden State.

First English edition published in 1981 by Colour Library International Ltd.
This edition is published by Crescent Books, Distributed by Crown Publishers Inc.
Illustrations and text © : Colour Library International Ltd. 163 East 64th Street, New York 10021.
Colour separations by FERCROM, Barcelona, Spain.
Display and text filmsetting by Focus Photoset, London, England.
Printed by Cayfosa and bound by Eurobinder - Barcelona (Spain)
Library of Congress Catalog Card Number: 81-67584
CRESCENT 1981

 Dep. Leg. B. 12.530/82